Mel Bay Presents

Electric Bass
for the Young Beginner

By Dino Monoxelos

CD Contents

1. Tuning the Bass (pg. 10)
2. Whole, Half, Quarter Notes (pg. 17)
3. Open Strings: Whole Notes (pg. 19)
4. Open Strings: Half Notes (pg. 19)
5. Open Strings: Quarter Notes (pg. 19)
6. Skipping Strings: Whole Notes (pg. 20)
7. Skipping Strings: Half Notes (pg. 20)
8. Skipping Strings: Quarter Notes (pg. 20)
9. Open Strings: Mix N Match (pg. 21)
10. Notes on the E String (pg. 23)
11. E String: Whole Notes (pg. 23)
12. E String: Half Notes (pg. 24)
13. E String: Quarter Notes (pg. 24)
14. E String: Mix N Match (pg. 25)
15. Notes on the A String (pg. 27)
16. A String: Whole Notes (pg. 27)
17. A String: Half Notes (pg. 28)
18. A String: Quarter Notes (pg. 28)
19. A String: Mix N Match (pg. 29)
20. Notes on the D String (pg. 31)
21. D String: Whole Notes (pg. 31)
22. D String: Half Notes (pg. 32)
23. D String: Quarter Notes (pg. 32)
24. D String: Mix N Match (pg. 33)
25. Notes on the G String (pg. 35)
26. G String: Whole Notes (pg. 35)
27. G String: Half Notes (pg. 36)
28. G String: Quarter Notes (pg. 36)
29. G String: Mix N Match (pg. 37)
30. Whole Rests (pg. 39)
31. Half Rests (pg. 40)
32. Quarter Rests (pg. 40)
33. Mix N Match Rests (pg. 41)
34. The Repeat Sign: Example 1 (pg. 43)
35. The Repeat Sign: Example 2 (pg. 43)
36. Exercises on the E & A Strings (pg. 45)
37. Exercises on the A & D Strings (pg. 45)
38. Exercises on the D & G Strings (pg. 45)
39. 3/4 Time Signature: Example 1 (pg. 47)
40. 3/4 Time Signature: Example 2 (pg. 47)
41. 3/4 Time Signature: Example 3 (pg. 47)
42. The Eighth Note: Example 1 (pg. 49)
43. The Eighth Note: Examples 2-4 (pg. 50)
44. The Eighth Note: Example 5 (pg. 51)

1 2 3 4 5 6 7 8 9 0

© 2010 BY MEL BAY PUBLICATIONS, INC., PACIFIC, MO 63069.
ALL RIGHTS RESERVED. INTERNATIONAL COPYRIGHT SECURED. B.M.I. MADE AND PRINTED IN U.S.A.
No part of this publication may be reproduced in whole or in part, stored in a retrieval system, or transmitted in any form
or by any means, electronic, mechanical, photocopy, recording, or otherwise, without written permission of the publisher.

Visit us on the Web at www.melbay.com — E-mail us at email@melbay.com

This page has been left blank
to avoid awkward page turns.

Table of Contents

Introduction 4

Choosing an Electric Bass...5

Parts of the Electric Bass 6

How to Hold the Bass 7

Left and Right Hands 8

Tuning the Bass..10

Tuning the Bass with a Piano 11

Tuning the Bass with an Electronic Tuner 12

Parts of the Staff 13

Open Strings on the Staff and on Your Bass..14

Whole, Half and Quarter Notes 16

Open-String Exercises 18

Notes on the E String (4th String) 22

Notes on the A String (3rd String) 26

Notes on the D String (2nd String) 30

Notes on the G String (1st String)..34

Let's Take a Rest 38

The Repeat Sign...42

Two-String Exercises 44

3/4 Time Signature...46

The Eighth Note or the 8th Note...48

Introduction

I first would like to say that this book was one of the most enjoyable books I've written. Music is a very important aspect of my life and I truly believe it is in most people's lives. Starting our children in a world of music at an early age is one of the most valuable things we can give our kids today. Music education is very important in our children's early years. Studies have shown that children that are involved in some sort of music program score higher in their daily school studies. Contributing to the music education of young ones is an absolute joy to me!

With that being said, I want to dedicate this book to my two beautiful daughters:

Samantha and Nicole
May both of you always stay young at heart

There are many beginner bass books available today but very few that are written with small hands in mind. I hope this book will fill that need. Although the notes haven't changed, the way we approach them has.

So let's get started.

Choosing an Electric Bass

This is the first and most important step in starting a child out on bass. There are many shapes and sizes of electric basses available today as well as string configurations; 4, 5, 6, 7, 8, 10, and 12-string basses. A four-string bass being the most common and what you should start your child with. Most basses are built in what is referred to a "long scale" which is usually about 34 inches from bridge to nut. There are medium-scale and short-scale basses too. These are what we want to look at depending on the child. Your local music store should be able to assist you in fitting a bass to your child. The child should be able to reach the headstock of the instrument easily without having to stretch his or her arm too far. Also remember that playing the electric bass is somewhat of a physical thing too, so be sure to find a bass that's easy to play and not one that may be too hard to play and discourage the student from wanting to play well.

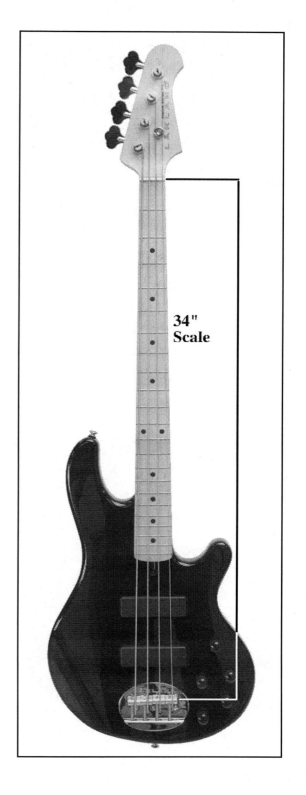

There are also a number of different parts that make up an electric bass. Some of them are necessary and some of them not. Looking at the pictures you'll see the basic parts of the bass. The most important parts being the body, neck, strings, and electronics. The bass in the picture shows two pickups and some extra control knobs. These are extras. As long as the bass you choose has at least one pickup and a volume knob, that is really all you need. Again, your local music store should be able to help you choose a proper instrument.

Speaking of this, there is one last thing that I think I should mention. In today's world of discount retail stores, mail order and internet sales, it's very tempting to look for the best deal when buying an instrument. Please do yourself and your child a favor and trust in your local store to purchase your instrument. Most store owners and their staff have been doing this a long time and have years of experience. Plus they will probably offer lessons as well as personalized service. They will be able to help you out regardless of your budget and in most cases can offer you the same deal that you would get from the huge discount retailer.

Parts of the Electric Bass

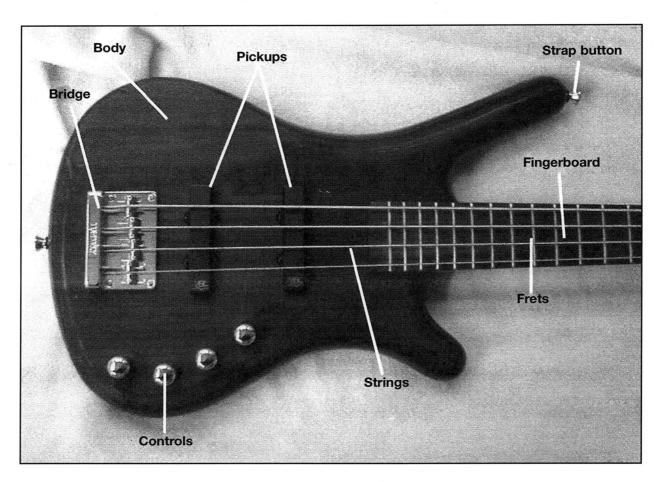

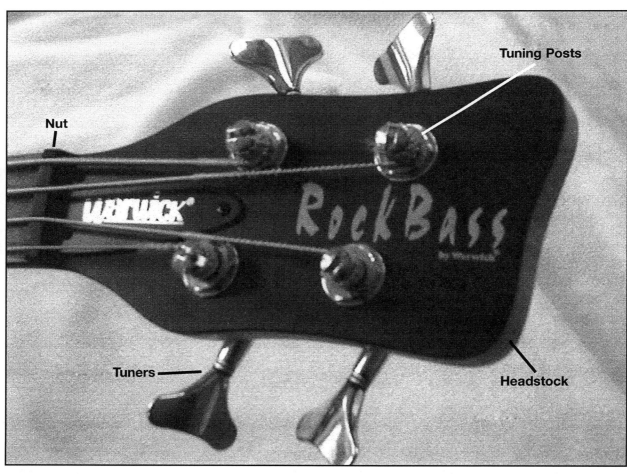

How to Hold the Bass

First off you should be seated in an upright position and not slouching. The bass should lie across your lap with the bottom cut-out resting on your right leg. The back of the bass should rest against your tummy and chest so that the instrument is sitting straight up (Fig. 1). Your right arm should rest over the top bout of the bass and support it from falling forward. Your right forearm should be hanging freely over the strings in a playing position (Fig. 2). Your left arm should extend out towards to the end of the neck but you shouldn't have to reach too far (Fig. 3).

The bass should be at about a 30 degree angle from the front of your chest (Fig. 4). It does not need to be completely parallel to your body.

If you decide to wear a strap, and you probably will, you want to adjust the length of the strap so that the bass hangs off of your body the same distance as it would if you were sitting. This is very important so that when you are practicing, whether standing or sitting, your hand positions do not have to be adjusted.

Fig. 1

Fig. 2

Fig. 3

Fig. 4

Left and Right Hands

Okay now that you've got the bass in a comfortable position lets talk about which hand does what.

Your right hand should be hanging over the strings somewhere around the pickups. This is the hand that is responsible for striking the strings and making them vibrate. There are a number of ways to do this. You can do it with a pick as seen in (Fig. 5) or you can use your fingers (Fig. 6). Using your fingers is arguably the most common method used. Especially your index finger and middle finger, also known as a two-finger technique. Whichever way you choose, just be sure to practice all the exercises in this book consistently with that technique. If you're using your first two fingers, be sure to alternate them back and forth. If you're using a pick, be sure to alternate between up and down strokes.

When you use your fingers, you simply want to drag your finger across the string to make it sound. Allow your finger to come to rest on the next string so you're using that string almost like a brake or a rest. You also want to rest your thumb on the top string or on the top of the pickup like in Fig. 6.

When using a pick, you want to rest the side of your palm along the top of the strings and use your wrist to move your hand up and down like Fig. 5.

Fig. 5

Fig. 6

Now that you've got the right hand working, let's take a look at what the left hand is doing. The left hand is responsible for fretting or holding the strings down against the frets like in Fig. 7. This is what gives you different notes on the bass. Take a look at Fig. 8. Let's notice a few things that are very important.

1. The hand is forming the shape of a C.
2. The wrist is straight in relation to the hand.
3. The thumb is resting on the back of the neck directly across from the middle finger.
4. The fingers are spread comfortably equal from one another.
5. The fingers press the strings down just to the left of the fret.

Pressing the string down just to the left of the fret is very important to achieve a nice, full sound without the strings buzzing against the frets.

Now the trick is to be able to pluck the strings with your right hand and fret the strings at the same time with your left hand. This takes some time and lots of practice so go slow and take your time to learn this right.

Fig. 7

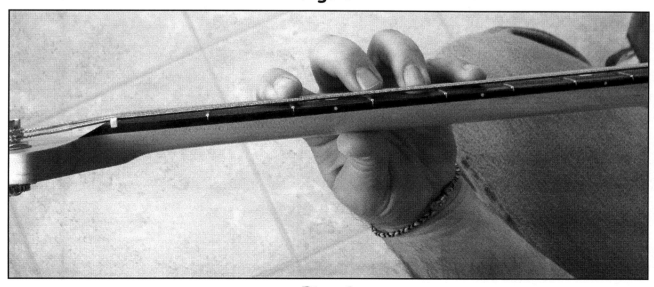

Fig. 8

 Track 1

Tuning the Bass

There are a couple of different methods used to tune a bass. Here we are going to look at the two most popular ones.

The first method is to tune the bass to a piano or keyboard (Fig. 10). The four open strings will have the same letter name and pitch as the notes that are shown on the keyboard. Now it is up to you to tune the string to the same pitch. Take a look at where each of the four notes rest on the staff too. We'll come back and explain this very soon.

The other method of tuning is to use an electronic tuner (Fig. 11). Most tuners will "hear" which note you are trying to tune to and then tell you by means of a little needle or lights how sharp or flat you are. Be careful using a tuner because sometimes if your tuning is way off, it might have you tune to another completely different note. If you choose to use an electronic tuner, it's best to have your teacher show you how to use it.

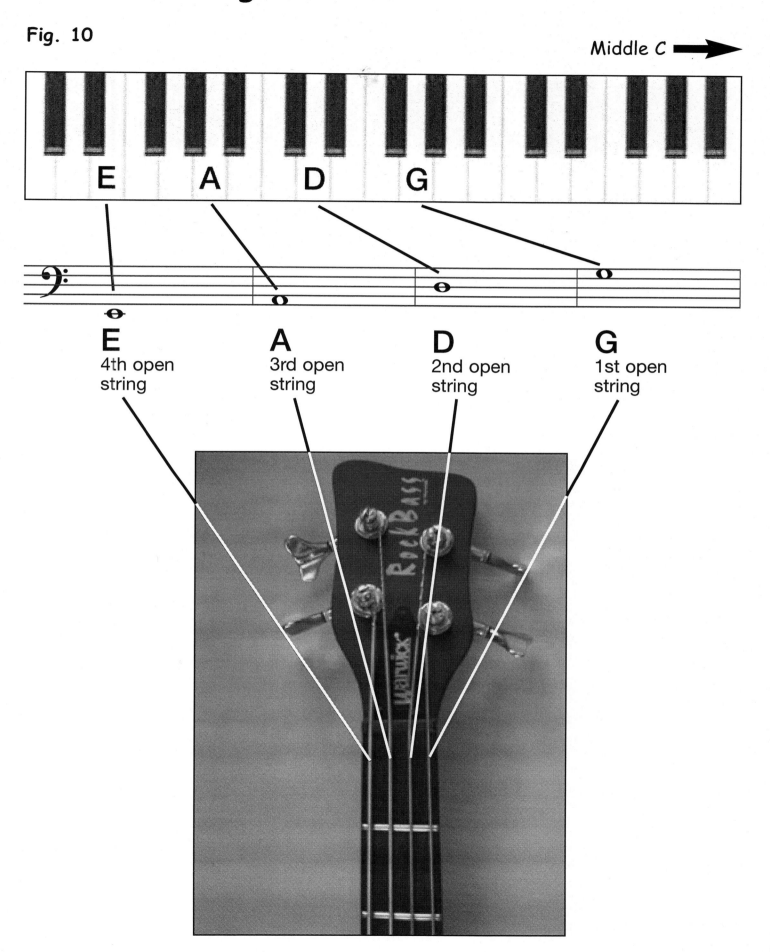

Tuning the Bass with an Electronic Tuner

Fig. 11

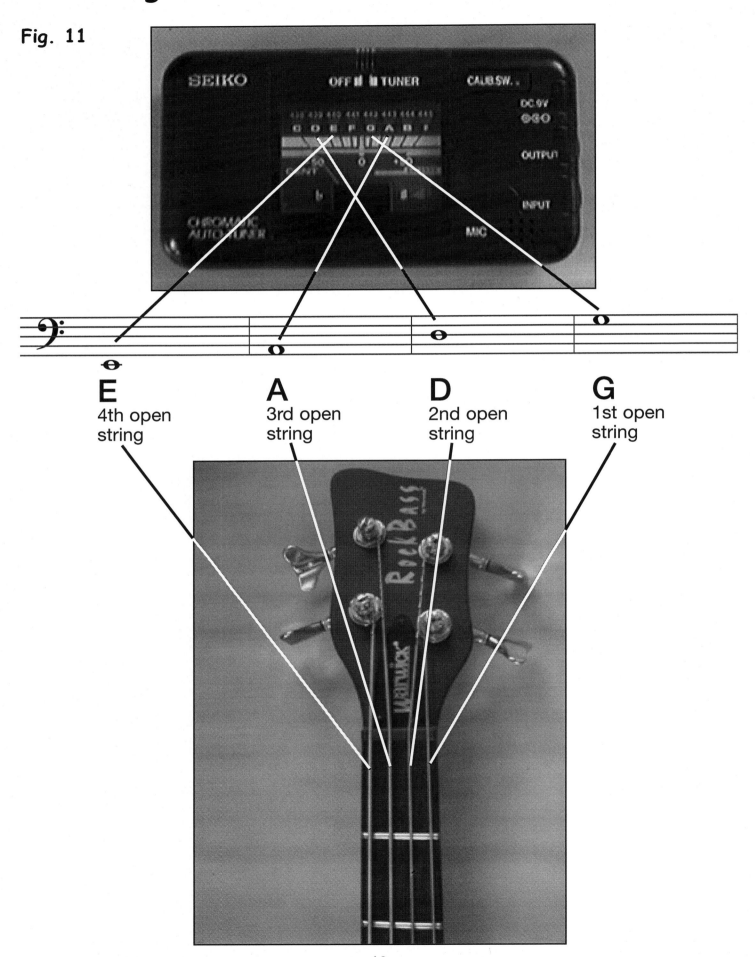

Parts of the Staff

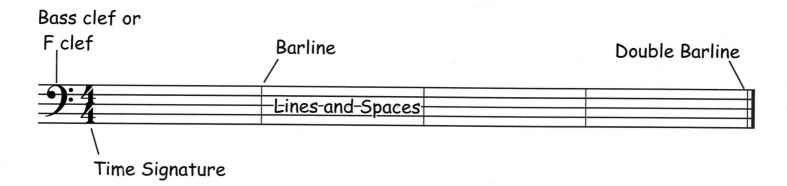

In this lesson we are going to learn about the parts of the staff. The staff is what you see above, with all the lines on it. This is very important because this is what we write our notes on and it tells us a bunch of information that we need to know when playing music.

The first thing we will learn is the **Bass Clef or F Clef**. This is the funny looking swirl mark at the very left of the staff. This is called the Bass Clef because it represents the register of our bass instrument. Other instruments might have a different clef at the start of their music but for us, our main concern is the Bass Clef. It's also called the F Clef because the line that the two dots sit above and below is the F line. Anytime we see a note on this line, we know it's an F.

The next part of the staff is the **Time Signature**. This tells us what meter of time we are playing in. Whether there are four beats to a measure or three or any other number for that matter. In this case, the top number 4 tells us that there are 4 beats to the measure which we will talk about a bit later as well as the bottom number.

The **Lines and Spaces** are where we put our notes and the notes tell us which pitches we will play and for how long on the bass. Each of these lines and spaces has a letter name that matches with the notes on your bass. We will be learning these very soon.

The **Barline** is what breaks the staff up into sections. Each section is called a **measure**. These measures are little pieces of time in which we play the notes. The **Time Signature** which we already discussed tells us that in each one of these measures, we will count four beats.

The **Double Barline** is the thick, double line that we see at the end of the staff. This tells us where the end of the piece of music is. When we see this, we know that this is the end of the music.

Open Strings on the Staff and on Your Bass

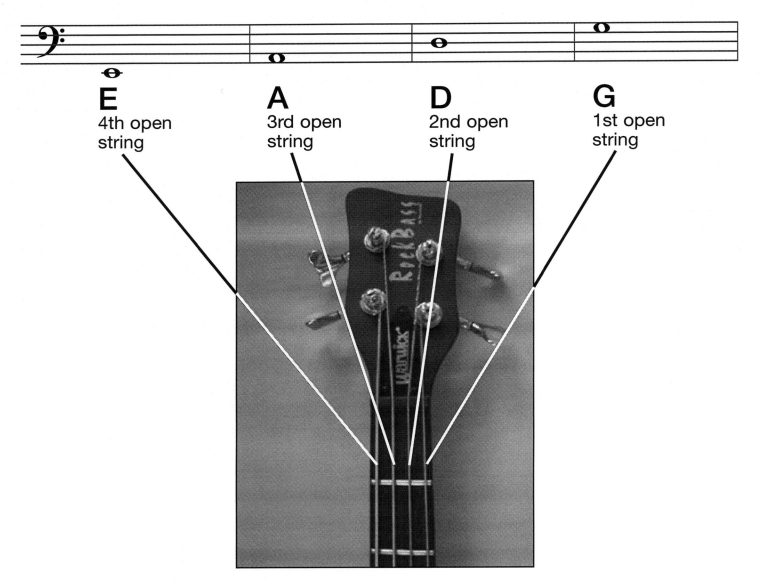

Okay now that we've got you all tuned up and ready to go, let's take a look at the open strings on your bass and how they look on a staff. You probably remember some of this from when we tuned the bass and the names of the open strings right? The first string that we'll look at is the G string and this is the bottom string as you hold your bass in the playing position. We'll call this the 1st string. The note for this string rests on the top or 4th space up on the staff. So whenever you see a note on that space, that means you will play that open string (G string).

The next string we will learn is the D string also known as the 2nd string on your bass. Take a look at where the note for this string sits on the staff. It rests on the 3rd line up on the staff. So, every time you see a note on that line, you will play that open string (D string).

The next string we will learn is the A string or the 3rd open string. Now take a look at where this sits on the staff. You'll see that is on the 1st space of the staff. So now anytime you see a note on that space, you'll know which open string to play. See how easy this is!

The last open string we will learn is the open E string or the 4th string. Now take a look at where this sits on the staff. Actually it doesn't sit on the staff at all does it? It's so low we have to make a line below the staff for it to sit on. This is called a ledger line. Anytime you need to write a line or space below or above the staff, we call it a ledger line. So now we see that anytime we have a note on the first ledger line below the staff, we know to play our open E string

Whole, Half and Quarter Notes

In this lesson we are going to learn about rhythm. Notes on the staff tell us two things; what notes to play on the bass and HOW LONG TO HOLD THEM. This is also known as rhythm. The way we write the notes on the staff tells us how long we are going to hold that note.

I've written each type of rhythm four times, one measure's worth for each of the open strings. As you learn each type of note, practice playing from one open string to the next.

Take a look at Example 1. This is what we call a WHOLE NOTE. A note is called a whole note because it takes up the WHOLE measure. A whole is worth 4 counts or 4 beats. So when we see a whole note on the open E string line like we see here in the first measure, we play that open string and let it ring out for 4 counts or beats as we call them. Then without stopping, we play the next whole note on the open A string space in the next measure and let that ring for 4 beats.

Try tapping your foot while you play this. Your foot should tap 4 times for each whole note.

Now take a look at Example 2. This is called a HALF NOTE. We call this a half note because it only takes up half of a measure. This means that a half note is worth 2 beats. So now we can fit two of these into each measure. When we play them, we count 1 – 2 for the first half note and then 3 – 4 for the second half note. So just like we did with the whole notes, we start on the open E string and play 1 – 2 then 3 – 4 so we play the open E twice in this measure letting each one ring for 2 beats. Then we move on to the next measure without stopping and play the open A string.

Last but not least let's look at Example 3. These are called QUARTER NOTES. A quarter note receives one beat or count each. So in this case each time you count 1-2-3-4, you will play one quarter note for each count in each measure and when you are finished with that measure move right on to the next measure.

Now that you know each type of note, practice these examples from top to bottom. Try to make the notes sound full and not run into each other. Remember what the left and right hands are supposed to be doing from the last lesson.

Whole, Half and Quarter Notes

 Track 2

Example 1 Whole Note

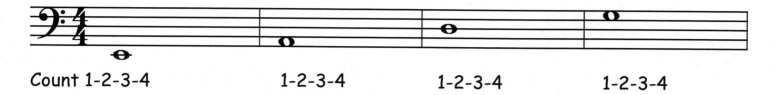

Count 1-2-3-4   1-2-3-4   1-2-3-4   1-2-3-4

Example 2 Half Note

Count 1-2   3-4   1-2   3-4   1-2   3-4   1-2   3-4

Example 3 Quarter Note

Count 1   2   3   4   1   2   3   4   1   2   3   4   1   2   3   4

17

Open-String Exercises

Okay, now that you've really learned all the open strings, let's play some music...

The first exercise is all whole notes on strings that are next to one another. Remember to count to 4 for each whole note that you play. Try this very slow at first.

The next exercise is all half notes on strings that are next to one another. This gets a little harder because now you have to count to 2 for each note. Be sure to play this slow and count for each note. Note: Try tapping your left foot for each count. This will help you keep the beat!!!!

Now let's look at the next example with all the quarter notes. Again, these are all on strings that are close to each other. Remember, each note gets one beat only so you should be tapping your foot for each note. Play this slow at first and then try picking up the beat.

So how did you do? By now you should have a really good idea of where the open strings are.

The next couple of exercises get a little harder because they aren't on strings next to one another. In other words, you have to skip over strings to get to the next string. Note: Try using your left hand to keep the other strings from ringing. This is known as muting the strings.

The first exercise is another whole note exercise that skips around so be careful not to let the other strings ring too much. Also be sure to hold each note for the full 4 counts.

The next exercise is all half notes. Again be careful because you have to move a little quicker to get to the next note. Watch out for those big string jumps.

Okay, this exercise is all quarter notes now. I made it a bit easier for you in the first four measures. You have to be careful though in the last four measures because it gets a little tricky where you have a different open string every two beats.

The last exercise here is very hard and I don't expect you to get it first off but if you practice hard and start off slow, you will be able to play this in no time at all.

Note: Try practicing one measure at a time. When you get good at one measure, move on to the next measure. Then try connecting the two measures and get them real good. Then move on to another measure. When you get that measure, add that to the first two measures.

Playing Strings That Are Close Together

Track 3

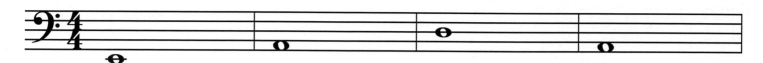

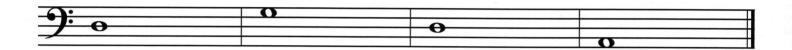

Track 4

Track 5

Now Try Skipping Strings!!!

 Track 6

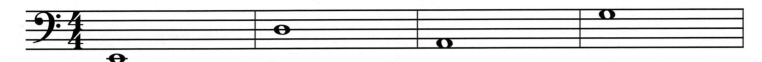

 Track 7

 Track 8

This is a Hard One!!!

 Track 9

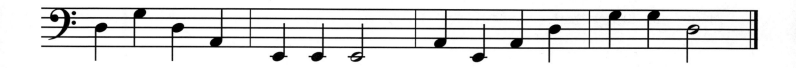

Notes on the E String (4th String)

Okay!!!! Now that we've learned to play all of our open strings, let's learn how to play notes on the fingerboard.

Let's take a look at the open E string. There are three notes we need to learn at first. So far we know that by playing the open string we are playing an E on the first ledger line below the staff. Now if we take our first finger and place it on the E string at the 1st fret, we will play F. That F note sits on the first space below the staff. Anytime we see a note here, we know to play the F on the first fret of our E string.

It is very important to watch the fingerings that I've written in.

Now let's put our 4th finger on the 3rd fret. Now we are playing a G. This G sits on the first line of the staff. Every time we see a note here, we know to play this exact G.

Now let's work through the exercises that I've written.

The first exercise is all whole notes. Be sure to play each note for a full 4 beats and keep your finger down on the string so that you don't get any weird fret buzzing sounds. If you do, adjust your fingers to keep the buzzing from getting loud.

Be sure to play these slow at first and then work your way up.

The next exercise is a half note exercise. This gets a little harder so be sure to look ahead if you can so you can see what note might be coming up next.

The next exercise is all quarter notes. Play this through slow at first and use the fingerings that you've learned. This will make it a lot easier too.

The last exercise is a very hard one. You should take your time to get this working. Try one measure at a time and keep adding measures as you get good at each one.

Notes on the E String (4th String)

 Track 10

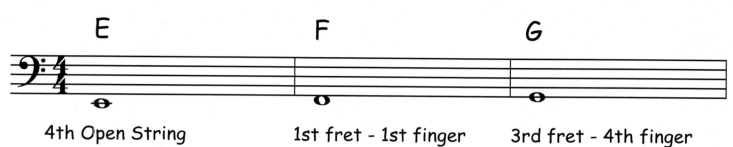

4th Open String   1st fret - 1st finger   3rd fret - 4th finger

Whole Notes  Track 11

Half Notes — Track 12

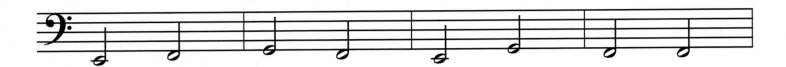

Quarter Notes — Track 13

Mix N Match  Track 14

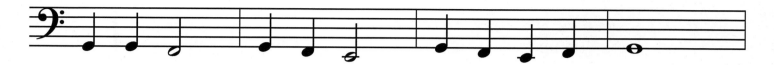

Notes on the A String (3rd String)

Hello and welcome to the A string!!!! This is the next door neighbor to the E string.

On this string we are going to learn three notes but you already know one of them and that's the open A. This note sits on the first open space of the staff.

The next new note sits on the second line up from the bottom. That note is B. Take a look at the picture and you'll see that it is the second fret on your A string. You must use your first finger to play this note.

The next new note is C. This note sits on the second space up from the bottom of the staff. To play this note, you need to put your middle finger on the 3rd fret of the A string, just like it is shown in the picture.

Don't worry about your 3rd finger yet, we'll have plenty for that to do real soon.

So whenever you see a note on the first space of the staff, you know to play the open A string. When you see a note on the second line up, you know to play the B on the second fret with your first finger. Then when you see a note on the second space, you know to play the C on the third fret with your middle finger.

Go ahead and practice through all of these exercises. Play them slowly at first and make sure you play them right. Don't try to rush through them. This is very important!!!!

Notes on the A String (3rd String)

 Track 15

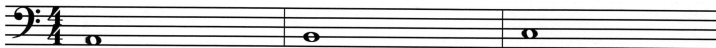

3rd Open String   2nd fret - 1st finger   3rd fret - 2nd finger

Whole Notes  Track 16

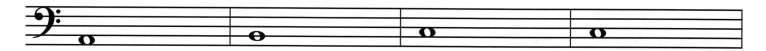

27

Half Notes  Track 17

Quarter Notes  Track 18

Mix N Match Track 19

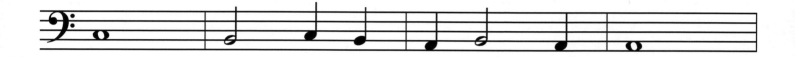

Notes on the D String (2nd String)

Okay, now that you've met the E and A strings, let me introduce you to the notes on the D string. We will learn three new notes just like we did on the E and A string. Of course you already know one of the notes so far.

The open D note rests on the third line up from the bottom of the staff, remember? Anytime you see a note on this line, you play the open D string.

The next note we will learn is E. This note sits on the third space up on the staff. Now this E is not the same as the E that you know as the open string. This E is what we call an "Octave" higher than the E that you've already learned, remember the one on the ledger line below the staff?

You want to play this E with your first finger on the second fret of the D string.

The next note is F. This note rests on the fourth line up from the bottom of the staff. You play this note with your middle finger on the third fret of the D string.

Go ahead and practice through these exercises on the D string and be sure to practice slowly and play all the notes correctly, giving each note its full value.

Notes on the D String (2ⁿᵈ String)

 Track 20

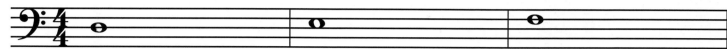

2nd Open String   2nd fret - 1st finger   3rd fret - 2nd finger

Whole Notes  Track 21

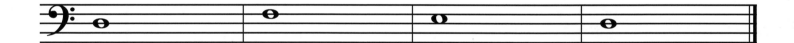

31

Half Notes Track 22

Quarter Notes Track 23

Mix N Match Track 24

Notes on the G String (1st String)

Okay kids, this is the last string we need to learn. After this, you should know all of the notes in the first five frets of your bass on all four strings.

Just like all of the open strings so far, you already know one of the notes on the G string. Yes you guessed it!!!! The open G. This note rests on the fourth space of the staff up on the top. We can play this note open.

The next note we need to learn is A. This note sits on the very top of the staff on the fifth line. You can play this note with your first finger on the second fret of your G string.

Now let's learn the B note. This note sits at the very tip-top of the staff right on top. We can play this note with our fourth finger on the fourth fret of the G string.

Remember to play through all of these exercises nice and slow and be sure to play good full notes without too many squeaks. You can do this by remembering to place your fingers just to the left of the fret you are pressing down on so that you can feel the side of the fret with the side of your finger.

Notes on the G String (1st String)

 Track 25

1st Open String   2nd fret - 1st finger   4th fret - 4th finger

Whole Notes  Track 26

35

Half Notes   Track 27

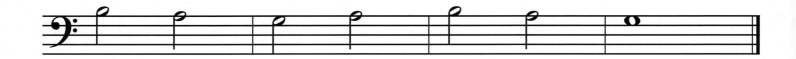

Quarter Notes   Track 28

Mix N Match  Track 29

Let's Take a Rest

Hey kids, now let's take a look something completely new. Remember how we have notes that tell us what note to play and for how long to hold them. Well we also have something called a rest. These are kind of like notes only instead of playing a note, they tell us not to play a note and to rest for a number of beats. Not playing a note is just as important as playing a note!!!

Let's take a look at the first rest.

This is a Whole Rest. Just like a Whole Note tells us to play for 4 beats, this tells us not to play for 4 beats. So any time we see this rest in a measure we have to be silent for 4 beats.

The next rest is called a Half Rest. This works the same way as the Whole Note did with the Whole Rest. A Half Rest tells us to rest or not to play anything for 2 beats. Just like a Half Note tells us to play for 2 beats, this tells us to not play for 2 beats.

The next rest is called a Quarter Rest. This works the same way as the Half Note did with the Half Rest. A Quarter Rest tells us to rest or not to play anything for 1 beat. Just like a Quarter Note tells us to play for 1 beat, this tells us not to play for 1 beat.

Go ahead and practice these exercises very slowly at first and be sure to have your teacher check you on these.

Remember, rests are very important in playing music so be sure to spend some time working on these.

Let's Take a Rest

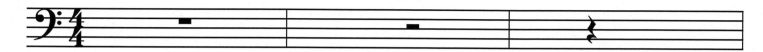

**Whole Rest:
Worth 4 Beats**

This is equal to a whole note only you rest instead of play.

**Half Rest:
Worth 2 Beats**

This is equal to a half note only you rest instead of play.

**Quarter Rest:
Worth 1 Beat**

This is equal to a quarter note only you rest instead of play.

Whole Rests  Track 30

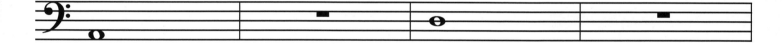

Half Rests  Track 31

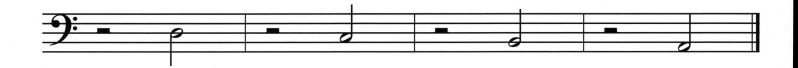

Quarter Rests Track 32

Mix N Match Track 33

The Repeat Sign The Repeat Sign The Repeat Sign

Okay, let's take a look at a musical sign that is very important. This is called the repeat sign. This is the funny-looking, double barline that has the two dots. I've circled them to point them out. You will sometimes see this at the end of a piece of music and it means exactly what it's called. You go back to a certain part of the music and repeat it all over again. Sometimes you go back to the very top of the music and sometimes you go back to the opposite facing repeat sign.

Take a look at Example 1. You will play all of the music (8 measures) and when you get to the end of the music where the repeat sign is, you will go all the way back to the opposite facing repeat sign (at the top), and play through the 8 measures one more time.

Example 2 is a little different. You play through the whole piece but when you get to the end, you only go back as far as the opposite repeat sign which is now at the beginning of measure 5. From here you just play to the end of the music one more time.

You will see repeat signs throughout the exercises in this book. Make sure to play them so you will get used to seeing them. Sometimes if the music is to be repeated more than one time you'll see a little notation at the top of the repeat sign telling you how many times to repeat like it is shown in Example 2.

The Repeat Sign

Example 1 Track 34

Example 2 Track 35

play 3 times

Two-String Exercises

Let's take a look at playing some more music now. These playing exercises will help you to get started being able to play music on two strings now instead of one.

Take your time with these and go slow. Make sure you play these correctly so that you don't develop any bad habits. Ask your teacher to help you through these.

The first example shows you how to play notes on the E and A strings. Practice this so that moving between both strings gets easier and easier.

The next example is the same exact thing only it helps you practice on the A and D strings. The music is pretty much the same as the previous example, it's just on the A and D strings.

The next example is again exactly the same thing only this time it's on the D and G strings. Again, be sure to go through these nice and slow.

Also make sure to play those repeat signs!!!!! They are there for a reason.

Exercises on the E & A String — Track 36

Exercises on the A & D String — Track 37

Exercises on the D & G String — Track 38

3/4 Time Signature

So far every piece of music we have worked on has been in 4/4 time, meaning that the time signature tells us that there are 4 beats to each measure. Now let's look at something a little bit different. A 3/4 time signature means that there are only 3 beats to each measure now. So instead of counting to 4, we are now going to count to 3. This gives a piece of music a whole new feeling to it.

The Dotted Half Note

Because there are only 3 beats to each measure now, a whole note will not fit because it's worth 4 beats. This is where the DOTTED HALF NOTE comes to play.

By placing a dot right after a note, you are adding one half of that note to itself. Sound confusing??? It really isn't. If you take a half note which is worth 2 beats and place a dot after it, you are now taking half of that half note, which is 1 beat and adding it to the 2 beats already in the half note. 2 + 1 = 3. Don't worry about the formula if it's confusing. Just remember that a dotted half note is worth 3 beats total.

Example 1  Track 39

Example 2  Track 40

Example 3  Track 41

The Eighth Note or the 8th Note

So far we have learned three different values of notes, the whole note, the half note and the quarter note. The smallest of these is the quarter note, which is worth one beat each. Now we are going to learn a note that is even shorter than the quarter note. It is called the EIGHTH NOTE, which looks like a quarter note only with a little flag on top of it.

An Eighth note is worth one half of a beat or one half of a quarter note. Remember how we count quarter notes? 1 – 2 – 3 – 4 right? One number for each beat or quarter note. Now we are going to cut those quarter notes in half and count the eighth notes as 1 – and – 2 - and – 3 – and – 4 – and. So each eighth note will receive either a number or an "and." When an eighth note receives a number, this just means that this is where the quarter note or DOWNBEAT is and when it receives an "and" this is the UPBEAT.

The easiest way to count notes is with your left foot. Each time you count a number or downbeat, your foot should be tapping down. Each time you count an "and" or upbeat, your foot should be coming up. This will take some time to practice but it is very important and should be practiced slowly. This will help you to develop great time and this is very important in being a great bass player.

Take a look at Example 1. This shows three different ways to write Eighth notes. The first way is in groups of beats and you'll see how the flags are beamed together. Beat one shows both eighth notes in it's grouping, then beat two, beat three, etc. Be sure to play through these counting 1 – and – 2 – and etc.

The next way is to write them individually with the flags separated. This is done when there is a need to break some groups up.

The last way is in bigger groups of two beats each where the flags are beamed for two beats each.

Examples 2, 3 and 4 are all open-string exercises that will get you started playing eighth notes. Practice them slowly and have your teacher help you through these. Be sure to remember to play the repeats too!!!!

Example 5 is a tough one but I know you can do it!!!!! This is a longer piece of music that really makes you concentrate. There are all sorts of things going on here. All of the notes you've learned as well as all of the note durations. Plus, don't forget the repeat at the end of the piece.

Practice this slowly and carefully. If you can get through this then you are well on your way to becoming a great bass player!!!!

The Eighth Note or the 8th Note

Example 1 Track 42

One and Two and Three and Four and
down up   down up   down   up   down up

One and Two and Three and Four and
down up   down up   down   up   down up

One and Two and Three and Four and
down up   down up   down   up   down up

Track 43

Example 2

Example 3

Example 4

 Track 44

Example 5 Hang In There

Biography

Dean "Dino" Monoxelos has been a bass player since the age of 13. Some 24 years later he's still perfecting his craft. Born from the James Jamerson and Duck Dunn school of playing, he relies on two very important fundamentals as a bass player, great feel and great tone! That, along with a good sense of humor, is something he instills in every one of his students. Having a working knowledge in most contemporary styles of music has also helped him along in his journey as a professional bass player. From Armenian Salsa to full blown Heavy Metal, he is at home in any style. He credits this to his love of all types of music but his true love is for R&B and Funk.

Born and raised in Dracut MA, Dino started out as many kids do, local garage bands and the high school jazz band where he was awarded the Louis Armstrong Award for Best Jazz Bassist. After playing the New England club scene for 10 years, Los Angeles became his next target. He went to Musicians Institute (BIT) in 1991 and after graduating, was asked to join the faculty. There he studied with Bob Magnusson, Putter Smith, Jeff Berlin, Gary Willis, Steve Bailey, Alexis Sklarevski, Jim Lacefield, and Tim Bogert to name just a few, and since he's been back in Boston, Bruce Gertz.

He's been around the world several times with various groups stopping mostly in Europe, Scandinavia and Japan. He has backed up players like Bernard Purdie, Efrain Toro, Maria Martinez, Doane Perry, Steve Perry, Brett Garsed, T.J. Helmrich, Debbie Johnson, Tiffany, Chasity Bono, Greg Bissonette, Keith Wyatt, The John Leite Concert Winds, The Pepperdine University Orchestra, and The Black Sea Salsa Band to name just a few. He is also one half of the acoustic variety act "The Carl & Dean Show."

He is the author of several books and instructional DVDs. He currently writes an instructional column for *Bass Guitar Magazine* titled "Bass Progressions" and is also a former instructional columnist for *Bass Frontiers Magazine*. He is an endorsing artist/clinician for Warwick Basses and Dean Markley Strings, conducting clinics in stores and schools around the country. Dino was recently spotlighted on Warwick's "Bass Survival 101" website as a featured artist. Dino is now the National Product Specialist/Clinician for Ampeg Amplifiers.

Dino also has numerous recording credits to his name too! *Gettup!* and *Red, Live from the Goodlife* Evan Goodrow, *Traces* and *Charade* Debbie Johnson, *C4* Catanine, *Landscapes of Christmas* Eddie Roscetti, and *She Just Wants To Be Loved* T.H. Culhane.

"Homesick" Southern Comfort, "A Path To Tollen" Mauro, Terry Nemeroff, Beto Lavato, Rolling Thunder, Dragonfly, and numerous demos and jingles.

Theater work includes musicals such as "Fame," "Violet," "Jesus Christ Superstar," "Joseph's Amazing Technicolor Dreamcoat," "Steel Piers," "Sweet Charity," "The Tribunal," "Working," and one of his personal favorites, "Batboy"! And, every year Dino is asked back to Pepperdine University in Malibu, CA to participate in the Pepperdine University's Songfest Orchestra. This has been a tradition for Dino now since 1994!